KU-408-469

This book belongs to

....

....

I am a reader and I celebrated
WORLD BOOK DAY 2024
with this gift from my local
bookseller and Puffin Books.

To my sister, for being stung by
a jellyfish all those years ago!
To my parents. Dad, for telling us those
stories when we were kids, and Mum, for
showing me I was capable of writing my own.
I know how excited you'll both be to see
one of my books in 'Savacentre'!

The CREATURES in our SOLAR SYSTEM and BEYOND

Can you GET Jellyfish in SPACE?

DR SHEILA KANANI

Illustrated by Liz Kay

PUFFIN BOOKS

UK | USA | Canada | Ireland | Australia
India | New Zealand | South Africa

Puffin Books is part of the Penguin Random House group of companies
whose addresses can be found at global.penguinrandomhouse.com

www.penguin.co.uk
www.puffin.co.uk
www.ladybird.co.uk

Penguin
Random House
UK

First published 2024

001

Text copyright © Dr Sheila Kanani, 2024
Illustrations copyright © Liz Kay, 2024

Design by Emma Wells, Studio Nic&Lou
Printed in Great Britain by Clays Ltd, Elcograf S.p.A.

The authorized representative in the EEA is
Penguin Random House Ireland, Morrison Chambers,
32 Nassau Street, Dublin D02 YH68

A CIP catalogue record for this book is available from the British Library

ISBN: 978-0-241-66983-9

All correspondence to:
Puffin Books, Penguin Random House Children's
One Embassy Gardens, 8 Viaduct Gardens, London SW11 7BW

MIX
Paper | Supporting
responsible forestry
FSC® C018179

World Book Day® and the associated logo are the registered
trademarks of World Book Day® Limited.
Registered charity number 1079257 (England and Wales).
Registered company number 03783095 (UK).

CONTENTS

INCREDIBLY, YOU CAN!

Even before we humans could travel off the surface of planet Earth, we have wondered what is up there – as well as who else might be out there.

To try and answer these questions, ever since spaceflight began we've sent all kinds of unusual things into the solar system – from animals like fruit flies and cockroaches to objects like musical instruments and gorilla costumes!

In this special World Book Day title in our Can You Get . . . in Space? series, you'll find out about all the animals and objects that have left our home planet.

We'll start with the smallest living creatures, working our way through to the biggest, while also meeting microscopic bacteria and a random assortment of objects that have been into orbit. You'll discover that a lot of things we take for granted on Earth are just *slightly* different when you're in orbit on the International Space Station. For example, did you know that large animals grow even BIGGER when they're in space?

We'll answer questions like 'How are animals trained for spaceflight?' and 'Could there be life on other planets?' And as the title promises, you'll find out what happened to over 2,000 moon jellyfish that went into space in the 1990s!

I hope you enjoy reading!

A NOTE TO OUR READERS

Perhaps now is a good time to mention that while no animals were harmed in the making of this book, using animals in experiments connected with spaceflight was commonplace in the past. Most of the examples of using animals that you will read about in this book are historical, and while animals are still used today in space travel, it doesn't happen very often. And when animals do make a trip into space now, their welfare is a key concern. The animals must be cared for in an environment that is in line with very strict animal welfare laws and standards, and there are many policies and regulations set out by the governments and authorities of the countries they are from that must be complied with before a trip into space can even be considered.

BUZZING
INTO
SPACE

FRUIT FLIES PAVE THE WAY

In 1946, fruit flies were the first creatures to be sent into space. Where these intrepid explorers flew, other insects and animals – including humans – followed later! Fruit flies and humans actually share many genes, so what we learned from the space-travelling flies in the 1940s gave us clues about the effects that a zero-gravity space environment and radiation might have on humans.

DID YOU KNOW?
Radiation in space is caused by extremely high energy particles that can move from one place to another. It can be harmful to the human body, which is why astronauts have to be very careful to be protected from it when they are in space.

The flies sent up to space in 1946 never came back, but in 1947 more flies went up in a V2 rocket, and they spent three minutes in space before coming home safely, with no evidence of harm from space radiation. If it wasn't for those out-of-this-world flies, we couldn't have sent monkeys into space in 1949, dogs in 1957 and, ultimately, humans in 1961.

IN THIS BOOK, WE'LL MENTION THE TERMS ZERO G (ZERO GRAVITY), MICROGRAVITY AND WEIGHTLESSNESS. BUT WHAT DO THEY MEAN?

Gravity is a force an object has that attracts another object towards it. The more mass the objects have – the more matter they contain – the stronger the effect of gravity will be. And the further apart the objects are, the weaker its effect will be.

The Earth's gravity attracts the moon to orbit – or go around – it. The Sun's gravity does the same thing to the Earth.

In space, gravity keeps everything 'sticking' together and orbiting around each other. For small objects far away from the Sun, its gravitational pull might be really weak. But it's hard to achieve zero gravity as pretty much everything has mass. And if it has mass, it exerts gravity. As far as we know, gravity never disappears entirely – it just gets weaker and weaker. Usually when people say zero gravity, they really mean microgravity.

Microgravity is when the effect of gravity becomes very weak, which could be because the object has very little mass or is very far away from another object. Microgravity is different from weightlessness because there is still a tiny force acting on the object.

Weightlessness is the feeling created when gravity is cancelled out by free fall. You might briefly experience free fall when you go on a rollercoaster.

WHERE DOES SPACE BEGIN?

OK, so we know that fruit flies were the first creatures in space – but how far did they actually have to travel to get there? The Earth's atmosphere extends way out into space, further than you might imagine. The exosphere is the highest layer of the atmosphere, and it starts at 10,000 km up. So where does Earth 'stop' and where does space 'begin'?

Well, it was decided in the 1940s, by the aerospace pioneer Theodore von Kármán, that the edge of space was the point where the air is too thin to produce effects like lift and drag. Lift is the force that presses upwards on a plane, in the opposite direction to gravity. Drag is the force that acts in the opposite direction to the plane's movement. At the point where the air gets too thin for these forces to be produced, gravity becomes the main force acting on the plane (or spacecraft).

Von Kármán set this point at 100 km above the Earth – which is now widely accepted as where space starts. But there isn't a fixed boundary between Earth and space. The US military awards pilots with their 'astronaut wings' – a special medal to show they've been to space – once they've flown 80 km above the Earth. Plenty of animals in this book would qualify for astronaut wings, although as far as I know none of them have been given a medal!

Aside from the famous fruit flies who buzzed off into space, have any other insects been there? And what about creatures like spiders and worms? Have they ever gone to space? Well, the answer is Yes, they have! NASA and other international space agencies have used all kinds of creepy crawlies in their space missions. So let's find out what these tiny beasts, despite being so different to humans, have taught us about spaceflight.

WHAT IS NASA?

NASA stands for National Aeronautics and Space Administration and is a part of the American government that was started in 1958. NASA is in charge of the areas of American science and technology that have anything to do with aeroplanes and space.

SPINNING WONDER-WEBS IN SPACE

Does a spider need gravity to be able to spin a web? Web spinning is just one of many things that gravity – and microgravity – might affect. So in 1973, NASA sent spiders into space, to find out, among other things, what the effects of the space environment might be on web spinning.

The first spiders in space were Arabella and Anita, who, once they'd adjusted to the conditions, began to weave perfect webs. Since then there have been dozens of spiders in space. Golden silk orb-weavers lived on the International Space Station (ISS), and photos of them weaving were taken every few minutes. Without gravity to tell them which way was up or down, the spiders appeared to use light to guide them as they spun their webs. This could be the reason why the space webs were more symmetrical than earthly ones.

In 2008, some spiders were taken up to the ISS, along with flies to feed them. One spider escaped, so there weren't enough left to eat the flies, which multiplied! Within about two weeks of launch, the flies started to cover the observation window of the tank they were in. Two weeks later, the window was so covered with flies that you couldn't make out the lone spider that was left!

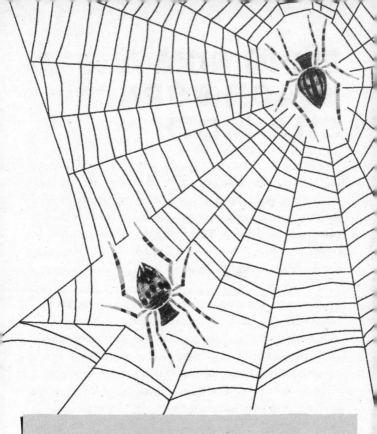

SPACE STATIONS

A space station is a spacecraft that is big enough for astronauts to live and work inside, and it is equipped to allow people to live on board for extended periods of time. Various space stations have been inhabited over the years, including Skylab and Mir, and most recently the International Space Station (ISS), whose construction started in 1998. Since then, over 250 people have lived on board the ISS, and for the past twenty-two years there have always been humans living in space!

FLOAT LIKE A SPACE-BORN SILK MOTH

Because they were so used to the pull of gravity on Earth, adult silk moths taken up to the ISS found it hard to fly in the microgravity environment. But those born on the ISS seemed to be already adapted to the space environment by the time they hatched, and were able to fly, float and sometimes even land with ease.

The Chinese space agency has done various tests with silkworms – the caterpillars of silk moths – which are able to spin and produce cocoons even in microgravity. Their silk fibres are tough and flexible, even in extreme conditions, and this could mean that silkworms might have a role in long-term space missions. So be prepared to share your spaceship seat with moth larvae in the years to come!

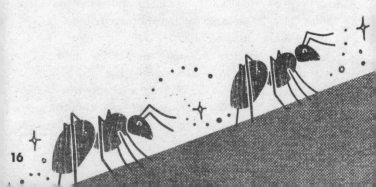

THE ANTS GO MARCHING INTO SPACE

In one mission, 800 ants were sent up to the ISS to help scientists study how ant colonies are affected by microgravity. Ants tend to search their environment and investigate different places in colonies – but how might they do this in a microgravity environment? After a few seconds of floating around, ants were able to grab themselves back on to surfaces. Sometimes they even used other ants as anchors! They also managed to flatten themselves against the surface of their habitat so they didn't float off. By comparing ant colonies on Earth and in space, scientists were able to see that space ants were still able to navigate, but were less effective in doing so than the earthbound ones.

SPACE HONEY FROM SPACE BEES

In 1984, NASA sent 3,400 honeybees into orbit to see if they could make hives in space. Despite the effects of microgravity, the bees were still able to build the wax honeycomb cells, and even the overall structure of the hives was similar to those on Earth.

Since bees appear to be unaffected by microgravity, they could be useful if we wanted to build communities on other planets, as they could be used to pollinate plants – and maybe even make space honey!

STOWAWAYS!

Apparently some insects have made it into space by accident – such as a Florida mosquito that hopped aboard a shuttle, and some rogue fruit flies that were found in the ISS. The mosquito was quickly squashed by an astronaut – after all, no one wants a mozzie buzzing about their ears, especially in the confines of a spacecraft!

HATCHING A SURVIVAL PLAN

Humans have long wondered about the possibility of life on a faraway planet. But in order to survive there, we would need to be able to reproduce wherever we landed. So far we've never tried to reproduce humans in space because it is simply too risky, but some animals have given birth aboard spacecraft – frogs, fish, quail, moths and newts, to name just a few! The first bird to hatch in space was a quail, which hatched aboard a spacecraft travelling to the Mir space station in 1990. It was soon followed by five brothers and sisters. To date, there have been no mammal births up there, as we need to understand more about the effect of microgravity on babies in space – but watch this space!

You've just learned that actual spiders have been sent to space – but did you know that there is a Spiderweb Galaxy up there too?

WHAT IS A GALAXY?

A galaxy is made up of billions of stars, planets and solar systems, as well as gas and dust. These stars are all influenced by gravity, each one of them orbiting around the centre of the galaxy. It is likely that there are billions of galaxies in the universe. Our solar system, including our star, the Sun, is in the Milky Way galaxy. The next closest big galaxy to ours is called the Andromeda galaxy.

THE SPIDERWEB GALAXY

The Spiderweb galaxy is in a group of stars called the Hydra constellation, about ten billion light years away from the Milky Way, the galaxy that we live in. The Spiderweb Galaxy got its name because it appears spider-like, catching other, smaller, galaxies in its 'web' of gravity. It also looks like it is in the centre of a cluster of galaxies, all smaller, that are merging together under the force of gravity. Because of the way it grows by trapping and eating its 'prey', the Spiderweb Galaxy is one of the most massive galaxies that we know about.

THE TARANTULA NEBULA

In one of our closest neighbouring galaxies, the Large Magellanic Cloud (LMC), we find the Tarantula Nebula. A nebula is a huge cloud of dust and gas where stars can form. This one looks a bit like a tarantula burrowing in its nest!

The Tarantula Nebula can be found in the constellation Dorado, and it contains more than 800,000 baby stars – including some of the hottest we have measured. The patterns created by the dust and bright patches in the nebula look like spider legs. And just like a tarantula, which is one of the biggest spiders on Earth, the whole nebula is huge. It stretches over 1,000 light years from one side to the other. It is so big and so bright that if it were positioned closer to us, it would be bright enough to cast shadows at night!

OF MICE AND MICROGRAVITY

FE, FI, FO, FUM, MEET MILDRED, ALBERT AND A CYLINDRICAL DRUM

So far, we've mentioned spiders and insects in space, but you might be wondering what the point was in sending such tiny creatures up to the ISS. Well, there is actually so much to learn from observing their behaviour in space – and on Earth too! But let's go a bit bigger now and talk about mice . . .

The first moustronaut flew in 1950. Then in 1951, eleven mice flew alongside Yorick the monkey – who you'll meet later in the book! In 1952, Mildred and Albert, two white mice, were flown up to space in a cylindrical drum that slowly rotated, allowing the mice to float about in a microgravity environment.

Many mice and rats were used in spaceflight before any human lives were risked. In 1958, the 'Mouse in Able' (MIA) project was launched, which tested mice with massive forces of up to 60G and as much as forty-five minutes of weightlessness. It was important to see how humans would be affected by more than 1G, but it was too risky to have carried out the tests on people at that time, so these heroic mice were used instead. Thanks to studies such as the MIA project, human astronauts are still trained with up to 20G to this day.

In 1972, Fee, Fi, Fo, Fum and Phooey were sent into space by NASA in Apollo 17. These mice circled the Moon seventy-five times, and they hold the record (along with the human astronauts on Apollo 17) for the longest time spent in orbit around the Moon, at 147 hours and 43 minutes, as well as for the most lunar orbits. To date, they are the last living creatures to have orbited the Moon.

DID YOU KNOW?

'G' is a measure of gravity, where G stands for gravitational force, or g-force. For example, the Earth's g-force is 1G (also written as 1g). 2G would be two times the force of Earth's gravity, and so on. The gravity on the Moon is equivalent to 0.166G, while the Sun's gravity is a huge 28G!

MICE AND NINETY-MINUTE SPACE DAYS

In 1973, mice were sent up to the Skylab space station to see how a microgravity environment would affect their circadian rhythm.

Your circadian rhythm is your internal clock. It is affected by daylight and darkness and other environmental changes, and it regulates how your body functions during a full day and night, over twenty-four hours. It affects how much you sleep, and when; the time of day when you have lots of energy; and the time when you might feel tired. If your circadian rhythm becomes messed up, this could cause you to sleep in the daytime, or you might find it hard to get to sleep at night.

To find out more about circadian rhythms and space, NASA sent a group of mice up to the ISS while keeping a set of genetically identical mice (the twins of the space group) back on Earth. Both sets of mice were given the same food for a whole year. The space mice experienced changes to their gut bacteria that the Earth mice didn't – changes that you might experience when you don't get enough sleep. However, the ISS mice seemed able to regulate their blood pressure, even though their circadian rhythm had been altered.

These findings are important because gut bacteria and blood pressure can affect the function of a lot of organs and systems in the body. So learning about how mice are affected in space can help astronauts prepare for any challenges they might encounter on a long mission – to Mars, for example.

Because the ISS is in constant orbit around the Earth, astronauts experience a sunrise or a sunset every ninety minutes. Waking up every ninety minutes would mess up their circadian rhythm, and if astronauts don't sleep properly, it could affect how they do their jobs and even put them in danger. But thanks to research such as the mice experiment, astronauts know how important it is to keep their circadian rhythms in order. Nowadays on the ISS, astronauts might use goggles to enhance or minimize their exposure to light, to trick their brain into thinking that it is experiencing daytime or night time.

HOW LONG IS A DAY?

The circadian rhythm of Earthlings is twenty-four hours, as a day on Earth is twenty-four hours long. But what if you were from another planet? Would your circadian rhythm be different? Yes, it would! A day on Mars is only slightly longer than one Earth-day, at twenty-five hours, and is called a Sol. But a day on Venus is 243 Earth-days long, and so is longer than a Venus year, which is only 225 days! One Mercury-day is 58.5 Earth-days, but a day on Saturn is only 10.5 hours long! Uranus is tipped over on its side by about 89 degrees, so it rolls rather than spins around the Sun, making 'day' and 'night' very confused – though it does take about seventeen hours to spin once on its axis.

THE MOUSE HOTEL

Taking lots of mice into space isn't easy. Rodent cages had to be adapted for microgravity – otherwise they'd be floating around in the space station!

In 2014, the Rodent Research-1 mission introduced a special 'mouse hotel' on the ISS. This permanent home for mice on board the ISS means they can take part in longer experiments, with comfortable living conditions.

Mice living in the mouse hotel have adapted rather well to life in space, as they can be housed in groups instead of individually. This reduces their stress levels and allows them to be sociable, huddling, feeding and grooming together as they do on Earth, with just a few small changes due to microgravity. For example, some space mice use their tails to anchor themselves to the floor. Others, though, apparently enjoy the effects of microgravity, running around in circles and bouncing off the walls!

MIGHTY MICE IN SPACE

In space, because of microgravity, muscle and bone degeneration – which means getting weaker – happens faster than it does on Earth. Thanks to the Mighty Mice in Space programme, scientists have found ways to prevent bone loss and keep muscles strong and healthy in space.

Some space mice were given a special drug to block muscle and bone degeneration, before being flown back to Earth. They were then compared with mice on Earth to see whether their muscle and bone mass had improved. The initial results showed that some of the space mice had been able to block the muscle and bone degeneration. This important experiment could help people on Earth who suffer from conditions like osteoporosis and muscular dystrophy that affect their bones and muscles.

On their return to Earth, the mice adapted back to 'normal' life very quickly. Mighty mice indeed!

MOUSE GALAXIES

Even though they are 290 light years apart, two spiral galaxies inside the constellation Coma Berenices – Latin for Berenice's Hair – have started to collide and merge into one another. They're called NGC 4676 and are also known as The Mice, or Mice Galaxies, because, at the point where they are colliding, both galaxies have grown a 'tail' of stars, gas and dust. Eventually these 'mice' will catch each other – the two galaxies will collide into each other completely and merge into one gigantic galaxy.

Scientists think that in seven billion years, our nearest galaxy, Andromeda, will collide with our own galaxy, the Milky Way. Will that pair of galaxies end up looking like two mice chasing each other too? Seven billion years is a long time to have to wait to find out!

DID YOU KNOW?

The rat is the first sign of the Chinese zodiac. Each of the twelve signs occurs every twelve years and is linked to a different animal. If you were born in the year of the rat, you are quick-witted, resourceful, smart, versatile and good at saving money! In which Chinese zodiac year were you born?

A GIANT LEAP FOR TORTOISE-KIND

TORTOISE PAIR WIN SPACE RACE!

Before opening this book, you might have heard about Neil Armstrong and Buzz Aldrin being the first humans to set foot on the Moon, in 1969. But I wonder if you knew that the year before, in 1968, two Russians actually beat them there?

The pair weren't humans, though – they were tortoises!

To date, twenty-four American astronauts have flown to the Moon, with twelve setting foot on it. But it was two Russian tortoises who got there first – the only 'non-Americans' to have gone to the Moon, and possibly the fastest tortoises in history. In order to leave the Earth's atmosphere, the rocket would have been going at 11 km a second, or 40,000 km an hour!

THE SPACE RACE

The so-called space race took place from the 1950s to the 1970s between the Soviet Union (known today as Russia) and the USA. The Soviets were the first to put a human into orbit around the Earth, but the USA quickly caught up by introducing its successful Apollo programme. The Russians were determined to 'win' the race by doing something incredible – something like putting a man on the Moon!

But there was a major setback to a Soviet Moon landing in 1967 when the cosmonaut Vladimir Komarov tragically died during his spacecraft's re-entry to Earth. The Russians became wary about sending any more humans into space and decided to shift the focus of their space programme on to something else. Tortoises.

Tortoises seem an odd choice when there are other more human-like mammals, such as chimpanzees. But the type of tortoise the Russians were planning to launch into space was quite small and therefore easy to secure tightly, and, conveniently, came from Central Asia, where the Soviet launch pad was.

In September 1968, the Zond 5 spacecraft was ready to launch. The intrepid duo, named '22' and '37', waited in the spacecraft for twelve days before it flew – luckily most of their life on Earth had been quite dormant anyway. For company, they had seeds, fruit-fly eggs, mealworms and bacteria, and a full-sized human mannequin in the pilot's seat!

The launch of their rocket was successful, and within three days the tortoises got their first glimpse of the Moon – the first Earthlings to see it up close and personal! They were whipped around the Moon by its gravity and then flung back to Earth, having spent just over six days in space.

During the mission, some of the star trackers failed – a bit like when your satnav/GPS fails to work and you get lost! This meant that on the journey back to Earth, the tortoises were not on the expected route and ended up experiencing a massive 20G before their spacecraft splashed down in the Indian Ocean. They were found after four days, and were recovered alive and well – though very, very hungry!

This mission provided the first high-resolution photos of the Moon and the Earth, and confirmed that living creatures could make a safe round trip to the Moon.

The Zond programme was meant to pave the way for Russian cosmonauts to set foot on the Moon, but the Americans beat them to it, successfully sending men to walk on the Moon just a year later.

Still, as amazing as putting men on the Moon was for NASA, they'll always know that two tortoises beat them to it. I only wish I could have flown past Zond 5 and glimpsed two tiny turtles floating about in microgravity!

DID YOU KNOW?

Russian astronauts are called cosmonauts. Cosmonauts and astronauts are the same thing, but cosmonauts are trained by the Russian space agency and astronauts are trained by, among others, NASA, the European Space Agency and the Japan Aerospace Exploration Agency. Nautes is a Greek word that means sailor, while astron means star and kosmos means universe. So cosmonauts sail the universe, while astronauts sail the stars!

WHY DOES THE MOON CHANGE SHAPE?

You may have glanced up at the Moon now and then and noticed that it changes shape. One night it's full, a few days later more of a crescent in the sky, and a while after that it's gone completely! How does it do that?

Well, the answer is that it doesn't really change shape or disappear. The Moon is always there – it just appears to change shape because of the way the Sun shines on it and because of how it moves around the Earth. The Moon's glow is actually light reflected from the Sun. As the Moon orbits the Earth, the Sun lights up different sections of it, making it seem like it's changing shape.

A full moon happens when the Earth is in between the Moon and the Sun, leaving the far side of the Moon in shadow and the side facing towards us fully lit by the Sun.

A new moon – when the Moon is fully in shadow, so we can't see it at all – happens when the Moon is in between the Sun and the Earth, so the side facing us is completely dark.

As the Moon slowly changes from a new moon to a full moon, it appears to be getting bigger, or waxing gibbous. When it goes the other way, from a full moon to a new moon, it appears to be getting smaller, or waning gibbous.

The Moon goes around the Earth roughly every twenty-seven days, but the Earth is moving too, so it takes the Moon just over twenty-nine days to complete its cycle. This is what we call a lunar month.

THE UNIVERSE ON THE
BACK OF A TURTLE

As far as I can discover, the Zond tortoises
have been the only tortoises in space, but
depending on what you believe in, we might all
be riding on the back of a giant turtle!

In Hinduism, the turtle is an avatar of the god
Vishnu, and on the turtle's back are four giant
elephants carrying the world.

A traditional Chinese creation story tells of a
giant turtle called Ao who props up the heavens
and makes sure the sky doesn't fall down.

For Native Americans, the Earth is a mound of
soil stacked up on the back of a great turtle.

Why do so many ancient cultures believe in
the turtle theory? Perhaps because the shape
of a turtle lends itself naturally to balancing
things on it. And maybe also because turtles, and
tortoises too, can live to a very old age, which
makes them seem wise and 'otherworldly'.

CAN YOU GET JELLYFISH IN SPACE?

INCREDIBLY, YOU CAN!

In 1991, NASA launched the Spacelab Life Sciences mission, which sent over 2,478 moon jellyfish polyps (sort of like jellyfish eggs) into space. The polyps were kept in flasks and bags full of human-made seawater that were injected with chemicals to feed them and help them reproduce. By the end of the study, NASA had 60,000 jellyfish in space!

The reason the jellyfish were taken into space was to see how the microgravity environment might affect how they grew, and what would happen to them when they came back to Earth. Even though jellyfish don't look very similar to humans, we both use gravity to go about our daily lives. So by learning about how jellyfish survive in space, we can learn more about humans too.

A BALANCING ACT

Us humans use parts of our inner ear to stay balanced and work out which direction is up or down. There are tiny crystals and hairs in our inner ears that move around and send signals to our brain, telling us whether we are up, down, left or right. We call this the vestibular system. Jellyfish have a similar system in their bodies, but the crystals and hairs are found in rings around the bottom of their mushroom-like part. When the jellies swim, the crystals roll around like marbles in a hoop.

DIZZY JELLYFISH

The main finding from this study was that the space jellyfish found it harder to swim once they got back to Earth. The scientists think they had extreme vertigo, which is like an intense feeling of dizziness. The crystals and hairs had all formed correctly in space, but scientists think the jellyfishes' nervous systems had adapted to space and couldn't readjust to life on Earth. In humans, vertigo is caused by problems in those hairs and crystals in the inner ear, meaning that funny signals get to the brain, causing the dizziness. So if human babies were ever born in space, they might feel a bit dizzy when they came back to Earth, or set foot on another planet!

MORE SWIMMING SPACE ANIMALS

Jellyfish aren't the only creatures that have been for a swim in space. Frogs, salamanders, sea urchins, fish and tadpoles have all taken the plunge! Many of them moved differently while in space – for example, fish and tadpoles were seen to swim in circles.

One special type of fish, called medaka, or Japanese rice fish, were sent into space because they have transparent skin, so scientists could see what was happening inside their bodies. The fish lost bone density, meaning their bones became weaker, which is something that would also happen to humans if they didn't exercise for two to three hours every day while in space.

In 1970, some bullfrogs were launched in their own spacecraft! Scientists wanted to see the impact of space travel on motion sickness, and the bullfrog has a very similar inner ear to a human. The frogs spent six days orbiting the Earth, and their vestibular system returned to normal when they got back home.

JELLYFISH GALAXIES

Jellyfish galaxies are types of galaxies that look – you guessed it! – a bit like jellyfish. The main disc of the galaxy is affected by pressure that pulls gas away from it, creating streaks of gas and dust that look like tentacles! One jellyfish galaxy, ESO 137-001, has a 'tail' of material stretching away from the main body that makes it look like it's swimming through space.

JELLYFISH OR UFO?

Another type of space jellyfish is formed during a rocket launch. When big rockets fly into space at dawn or dusk, plumes of gas that come from underneath the rocket are lit up by sunlight and can look like a giant glowing jellyfish hanging in the sky. This happens because although it's dark on the ground before sunrise or after sunset, the gas from the rocket travels high enough to be lit up by the Sun's rays, so the observers on the ground see the gas illuminated against the dark sky. These space jellyfish look different depending on where you are when you see them, which is also true of rainbows. Some people have seen these space jellies and thought they were unidentified flying objects!

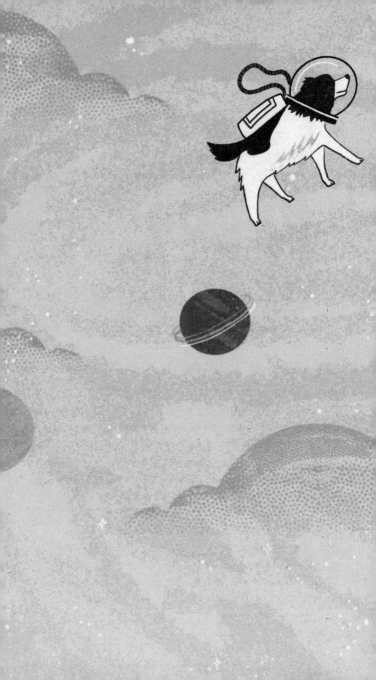

FOUR-FOOTED FRIENDS IN SPACE

WALKIES TO THE STARS

The first dogmonauts were Tsygan and Dezik, Soviet dogs who made it into space in 1951, after completing six months of training. They were shot up 110 km into space in a small cabin and came back down again within fifteen minutes. They experienced many times the force of gravity and landed back on Earth with the aid of a parachute and a bump! Both pups trotted out of the cabin completely unharmed, as if they'd just been for a walk in the park.

UNLUCKY LAIKA

In 1957, the Russian satellite Sputnik 1 made history as the first human-made object to orbit the Earth. Sputnik 2, launched later the same year, was six times heavier because of its special passenger – a stray dog called Laika who became the first creature to orbit the Earth and to spend more than three minutes in space.

The Russian space agency had picked a group of female street dogs to train them to be space dogs. They chose female dogs because they are generally smaller – and therefore lighter and cheaper to fly – and more obedient than male dogs. And they thought stray dogs were more likely to be resilient – if they could survive the harsh Soviet streets, then hopefully they could survive anything . . .

The dogs went through a set of tests, including living in tiny capsules for weeks at a time, until eventually there was only one left – poor little Laika (Russian for 'barker'). *Why poor?* you might ask.

Well, while she had the fame of being the first dog to orbit the Earth, unfortunately Laika's survival was never part of the plan. However, her sacrifice on a one-way mission to space led to great improvements in future space missions with animals on board. We all thank you, Laika!

There are statues commemorating Laika at the Russian cosmonaut training facility called Star City – as well as a series of stamps with her face on them!

DOGGY DUO'S DAY OUT IN ORBIT

A few years later, in August 1960, Belka and Strelka, two more stray female dogs, were chosen for the Soviet space programme. These two made it back to Earth in one piece after orbiting around the planet for a whole day. On board their spacecraft were also several plants, fungi (mushrooms), many flies, one rabbit, two rats and forty-two mice!

Although the fruit flies survived their mission in 1947, this motley crew of unusual astronauts were the first Earthlings to return alive after orbiting the Earth. Not long after her out-of-this-world journey, Strelka even gave birth to puppies. One of them – called Pushinka ('Fluffy') – was gifted to John F. Kennedy, the president of the USA.

By the time Yuri Gagarin became the first human in space, in April 1961, there had been forty-eight dogs in space, and since then there have been even more. Other dogmonauts include Zvyozdochka ('Starlet'), who orbited Earth just once along with a wooden dummy, in a practice mission for human spaceflight; and Veterok and Ugolyok, who spent twenty-one days in orbit, living longer in space than any human had at that time.

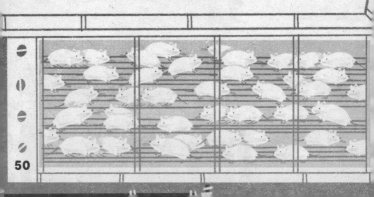

ARE YOU FELINE LEFT OUT?

If you're more of a cat person, you might be wondering where all the cats in space are . . .

Well, cats were also trained for space, but dogs were more often chosen as it's easier to train them. A cat named Flamengo was supposed to go into space aboard a rocket built by students at a Brazilian Army technical school, but this project was cancelled because animal-rights activists didn't agree with it. Flamengo was a pet belonging to the daughter of the lieutenant-colonel leading the project, and even though Flamengo never got his astronaut wings, he became a Latin American celebrity.

The French space programme managed to train fourteen cats to go into space – but in the end only one, Félicette, made it. Like the Russian dogs, Félicette was a stray, who was brought in from the streets specifically for training and testing. She was eventually chosen over the other thirteen cats to fly to space because she was a good weight and very calm. The intrepid feline was launched into space in 1963 and spent thirteen minutes up there before safely returning to Earth.

Félicette's bravery was recognized with a special stamp with her face on it, and a statue of her is now housed at the International Space University in France.

DOGS ON MARS?

The idea of taking your pet to Mars might sound cool, but we're a long way off from setting foot – or paw – on the red planet. But although there aren't concrete plans to send real dogs to Mars, NASA scientists have recently presented a 'Mars Dog' named Au-Spot to the space community. This is a four-legged robot that would be able to avoid obstacles, choose its own path, navigate difficult terrain and make its way down into the underground caves on Mars – all without needing a human to be there to take it for a walk!

This robot dog could travel much faster than a real dog and could also fall down and get back up by itself. Plus, it would be unaffected by the natural radiation on the surface of Mars, which would be dangerous for an Earth dog within minutes. Using laser pulses, thermal imaging and motion sensors to investigate Mars, Au-Spot could pave the way for human exploration, just like Laika and all the other dogmonauts did in the early years of space travel.

DOGGY CONSTELLATIONS

Humans have seen patterns and shapes among the stars for thousands of years. Some of these groups of stars, or constellations, are thought to resemble animals, mythical creatures and inanimate objects. Today, there are three 'official' doggy constellations, plus a few doggy stars!

YOU CANNOT BE SIRIUS!

The amazing thing about Sirius, the Dog Star, is that it isn't one star – it's two! Sirius A and B form something called a binary star system, that shines brighter than any other star in the night sky. Sirius is about twenty-five times brighter than our Sun, but because it is so far away from us it seems to be dimmer.

Sirius is also known as the Dog Star because it is part of the constellation Canis Major (Latin for 'greater dog'), which is said to be the hunting dog of Orion, the constellation named after the Greek god of hunting. If you look at star maps you will see the dog chasing the hare constellation Lepus, which is located beneath Orion. The other canine constellations are Canis Minor ('lesser dog') and Canes Venatici ('hunting dogs').

For the ancient Greeks, when Sirius rose in the sky it marked the 'dog days' of summer, when it became so incredibly hot that even dogs wouldn't go outside.

The opposite was the case for the Polynesians, who lived in the southern hemisphere. When they saw Sirius, they knew that, for them, winter was coming.

Chinese astronomers (people who study planets and stars) called Sirius Tian Lang Xing, the celestial, or sky, wolf.

And it's not just stars that are named after man's best friend. An asteroid called 1865 Cerberus and Kerberos, the fourth moon of Pluto, are both named after Cerberus, the three-headed dog who guards the entrance to the Greek underworld.

HOT DIGGITY DOG!

Did you know that there are also hot DOGS in space? These aren't sausages that astronauts can grab to eat on the go, but hot Dust Obscured Galaxies (DOGs) – galaxies that are thousands of times hotter than our Milky Way and bursting with stars! They can't be seen through optical telescopes due to their high levels of dust.

MONKEYS
IN SPACE

ALAS, POOR YORICK

More than thirty monkeys and apes have been into space. Although the Russians thought that monkeys might be too hard to train, NASA favoured monkeys over dogs because of their human-like qualities. The very first monkey in space, in 1949, was called Albert II and he went 134 km up into the atmosphere.
In 1951, Yorick, accompanied by eleven mice, became the first monkey to survive spaceflight – though sadly only for two hours.

The first monkeys to survive spaceflight and return alive and unharmed were a rhesus monkey named Able and a squirrel monkey called Miss Baker, in 1959. Miss Baker managed to withstand a massive 38G during her space journey, with no obvious impact on her body on her return to Earth. She lived to the ripe old age of twenty-seven and is buried at the United States Space and Rocket Center in Huntsville, Alabama.

NASA soon started working with chimpanzees, as they are even more closely related to humans than monkeys. Like humans, chimps are intelligent and have emotions and thought processes. They could also perform tasks during a space mission, which was an important step towards proving that humans could eventually go into space and operate spacecraft.

MONKEYS OR APES?

Apes, such as chimpanzees, and monkeys are both primates, but they have many differences. Monkeys have tails, which they use to swing through trees, while most apes do not have tails and are more comfortable on their hind legs. Apes have less hair, especially on their faces, and their chests are usually wider and broader. Apes are generally smarter than monkeys and can use communication methods such as body language and sign language.

HAM IN SPACE

The first ape in space was a chimpanzee named Ham.
He was first called Chang, but when he was taken to the
Holloman Air Force Base in New Mexico, he was renamed
'Holloman Aero Medical', or HAM.

To prepare for spaceflight, Ham went through g-force
training – which means being exposed to forces stronger
than Earth's gravity. He also had to adapt to long periods
of time strapped to a chair and was taught to pull levers
when he saw blue lights flash.

After eighteen months of training, in 1961 Ham was sent
into space at the age of three and a half. He was able
to perform the set of tasks assigned to him successfully,
pulling the levers like he'd done back on Earth. His
reaction times in the microgravity environment of space
were found to be only slightly slower than on Earth.
Ham's success proved that humans would be able to do
tasks in space as well.

FLOATING AROUND THE SPACE STATION

Because the space station travels at very high speeds in order to counter the pull of Earth's gravity, passengers travelling in it may experience a feeling of weightlessness, as though they're moving in slow motion. If you gently pushed one side of the spacecraft, you would float and glide across to the other side. But if you pushed too hard, you might bounce off the sides of the room like a rubber ball!

This is all down to Sir Isaac Newton's third law of motion, which says that every action has an equal and opposite reaction. In other words, every time you move in one direction, an opposite force is created, so if you were floating in the centre of the room and you threw a ball forward, you would move backwards.

The result of all this is that humans and chimps find doing tasks in space much easier than doing them on Earth – just slower. Heavy objects can be easily shifted with your little finger. For this reason, chimps like Ham would have found it easier – but slower – to do their lever-pulling tasks once they were in space.

HUMANS BOLDLY GO INTO SPACE – FOLLOWED BY A CHIMPANZEE . . .

On 12 April 1961 and 6 August 1961, the Soviet Union managed to send the first humans into outer space.

But although Yuri Gagarin and Gherman Titov both orbited Earth for a full day, NASA was still not 100% happy with the safety of spaceflight for humans. The Americans were particularly concerned with weightlessness and being in a small, confined cabin for any length of time. So later that year, they sent Enos into space instead, making him the first chimpanzee to orbit the Earth.

Enos experienced 8G and weightlessness on his space journey. He had to pull levers to turn off lights and complete other short tests to check whether his brain was functioning properly in microgravity.

YET MORE MONKEYING AROUND IN SPACE

The Russians did also send some more monkeys into space (mainly rhesus monkeys), and in 1967 even the French sent pig-tailed macaques into suborbit. NASA kept sending monkeys into space until the 1990s, when animal-rights groups put pressure on the space agency to stop using monkeys in this way.

Today, NASA and the Russian space agency no longer use monkeys or apes in their testing, switching back instead to smaller animals like mice and insects. These small creatures can also help us to learn more about human spaceflight, but they are easier to take care of, and they occupy less space!

MONKEY HEAD NEBULA

You've heard about the monkeys and apes in space –
but what about nebulas that look like monkeys?

The Monkey Head Nebula – also known as NGC 2174 –
is a region where new stars are born, and it can be
found in the Orion constellation. It is mostly made up of
hydrogen gas and is called an emission nebula because
it emits ultra-violet (UV) light. The newly formed stars blast
dark dust streams away from the centre of the nebula. It's
this mixture of dust and UV light that creates the nebula's
monkey-head shape. Though when I glance at it, I see a
bearded man, not a monkey! Look it up on the internet . . .
What do you see?

NGC 3199, found in the Carina constellation, is also
an emission nebula. It has a bow-like shape, which
has given it the nickname 'the Banana Nebula'. If it's
anywhere near the Monkey Head Nebula, it might end
up as a starlight snack!

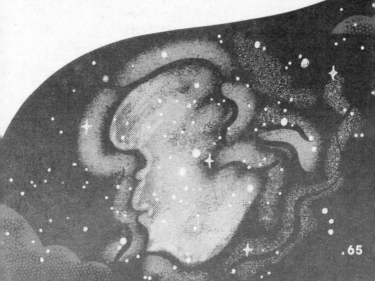

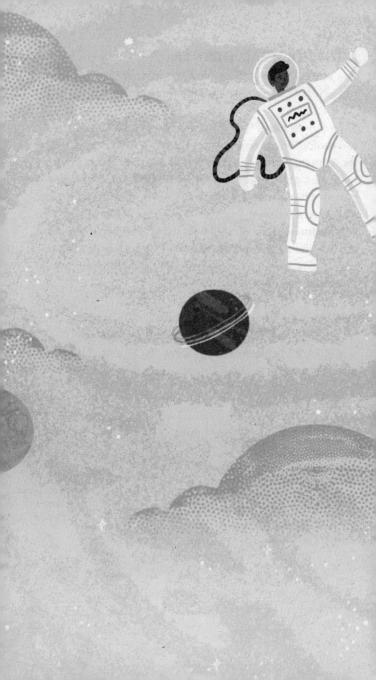

HUMANS TREK TO THE STARS

TICKET TO RIDE IN SPACE

Since Yuri Gagarin first blasted off into space in 1961, around 600 humans have trained to be astronauts. A month after Gagarin's mission, Alan Shepard became the first American in space. The first woman in space was Valentina Tereshkova in 1963; the first American woman was Sally Ride in 1983; and Alexei Leonov carried out the first spacewalk in 1965.

To date there have been twelve American men on the Moon (between 1968 and 1972). Neil Armstrong and Buzz Aldrin were the first to set foot on the surface in 1969 on the Apollo 11 mission.

The first Indian citizen in space, in 1984, was Rakesh Sharma (flying with the Russian space programme), while the first British person in space, in 1991, was Helen Sharman (also flying with the Russian space programme).

In 2001, a new type of astronaut was born – the space tourist! Dennis Tito was the first person in space who had paid for his ticket to train as an astronaut and go into space. He spent eight days on the ISS.

And history keeps being made! In 2003, we saw the first Chinese astronaut, Yang Liwei. The NASA Artemis missions plan to land the first woman and the first person of colour on the Moon as early as 2025. Watch this space!

LEARNING TO FLOAT

The training given to human astronauts to prepare them for weightlessness includes:

· Hours of classroom lessons, team-building exercises and training to learn how to handle equipment in space.

· Centrifuge experiments – a centrifuge is a small pod at the end of a long mechanical arm. The astronaut sits in the pod and is spun round and round. The spinning sensation exerts extra G on their body, helping them learn how to deal with these strong forces.

· Flying on the 'vomit comet' – an aeroplane that flies in a parabolic path, which means it flies very steeply up, and then very steeply down (one parabola). On the up part, the astronaut will feel additional g-force. On the way down, they will feel weightless.

· Neutral-buoyancy training sessions, a bit like scuba diving, in a huge swimming pool, wearing special weighted swimwear and walking underwater using life-sized models of space vehicles. Being underwater is about the closest experience to weightlessness that we can create on Earth. These training sessions might last seven hours at a time! Just think how tired you are after your swimming lesson, and then imagine how tiring this training would be . . .

· Exercises on the precision air-bearing floor, which is like a giant air hockey game, allowing astronauts to practise moving huge objects by sliding them around on a smooth metal floor that has air forced through it.

TWINS LIVING APART

NASA carried out an interesting experiment using a pair of identical twins, Scott and Mark Kelly, both trained astronauts. In 2015, Scott lived on the ISS for one year, while Mark acted as the control on Earth. You might know from doing your own science experiments that it's useful to have a control for comparing your results with. Identical twins share the same genes, which makes them ideal for experiments; when researchers change the environment for just one twin, they can see how it impacts their body by comparing against the other twin.

In this experiment, science teams studied the twins' genes, brains and bodies before, during and after their year apart, and the results revealed that living in space for a long time can affect mental reasoning, memory and immune systems. After spending a year in space, Scott said it took him another eight months to feel 'normal' again.

Although the twin experiment didn't reveal anything really alarming, it did show us that humans are definitely not adapted for long-term life in space, in zero-gravity conditions.

HUMANS AND MICROGRAVITY

So, what does happen to humans in a microgravity environment? Our bodies have evolved on Earth, where gravity is measured as 1G of gravitational force exerted on us at all times. If you change the strength of that gravity, or if you take it away completely, the human body reacts in ways we might not expect. By doing physical experiments on astronauts and by monitoring their daily lives and functions, we might be able to learn what the effects of gravity – and microgravity – are on the human body, and we might even be able to use our knowledge to make medical advances here on Earth.

PUFFY AND STUFFY IN SPACE

It takes astronauts a few days to acclimatize – or get used to their environment – when they first reach space. The microgravity environment causes bodily fluids to shift and pool in other places, so their faces might look puffy and their noses might feel stuffy.

Day-to-day life on board the microgravity environment of the ISS – where there is no 'up' and 'down', and no 'top' and 'bottom' – includes spacewalks to fix any parts of the spacecraft that aren't working properly, two to three hours of exercise per day to keep astronauts' bones and muscles strong, and carrying out scientific experiments – such as trying to grow plants in space!

SLEEPING IN SPACE

Going to bed on the ISS involves tying yourself into your sleeping bag and attaching yourself to a wall – and wearing an eye mask to avoid being woken up every time the ISS orbits Earth.

In space, the carbon dioxide that you breathe out is weightless and it forms a 'bubble' around your head. Funny as this might seem, it could suffocate you, so astronauts make sure that their wall-mounted sleeping bag is next to a fan, so that the air circulates well.

EATING IN SPACE

On the space station, food is pretty different from what you'd eat on Earth – astronauts can't just pop to the shops! Uncrewed cargo ships such as the *Cygnus* bring supplies of fresh fruit and veg every few months, but in the meantime astronauts rely on freeze-dried foods that can be rehydrated.

You can't have bread in space because the crumbs would go everywhere, so if you want a sandwich you'd need to use a tortilla or chapati instead. Tim Peake chose a bacon sandwich as his first meal in space, but he had to have bread with no crusts that came from a can!

Drinks can't be consumed from open containers as the liquid would just float off, so everything, even coffee and tea, is drunk from a pouch, using a straw.

Astronauts can take certain treasured items with them, and, in 2015, the Italian astronaut Samantha Cristoforetti chose to take a coffee machine into space.

In the microgravity environment on the ISS, your senses of taste and smell can be affected. Whereas on Earth, gravity pulls fluid down into our legs, in space it isn't dispersed, and can block nasal passages and stop astronauts from smelling well. This can affect the taste buds too, so food in space tends to be made with as much flavour as possible – with lots of garlic, and chilli sauce always to hand!

WASHING IN SPACE

In microgravity, liquids behave differently from how they behave on Earth. Blobs of liquids can grow much bigger in space, and they move much slower than they do on Earth. Fire, too, looks different, with spherical (meaning round like a ball) flames because the heated air doesn't move in the same way as it does on Earth.

Washing hands, brushing teeth, showering and dressing are all different in space. Astronauts wash using a pre-mixed pouch of soap and water, and if they squirt it out of the pouch, the ball of shower gel floats around! To wash your hands, you grab the ball, then wipe it off with a towel. Other methods include using cloths with the soapy water mixture already infused into them – in other words, giant baby wipes! I bet they are quicker than having a shower, though. Although if you are living with the same five people for six months, none of you need to worry too much about how you smell . . .

When you were learning to brush your teeth as a young child, you might have been taught not to swallow the toothpaste, but instead to spit it out. It's not like that in space, though . . . In order to rinse your toothbrush, you have to suck up a bit of water, and then wash it around your toothbrush in your mouth, before swallowing the toothpaste and the water so you don't have globs of toothpaste floating around the spacecraft.

What on earth would you pack for a trip to space?

If astronauts are planning on spending six months in space, this is what their luggage might contain:*

- ☑ Sports shoes for exercise

- ☑ 60 pairs of sports shorts (1 pair for every 3 days of exercise)

- ☑ 60 sports T-shirts (1 for every 3 days of exercise)

- ☑ 60 sports bras (1 for every 3 days of exercise)

- ☑ 18 work tops or shirts (1 for every 10 days)

- ☑ 18 work T-shirts (1 for every 10 days)

- ☑ 18 pairs of work trousers (1 for every 10 days)

- ☑ 2 jumpers

- ☑ 2 pairs of overalls

- ☑ 90 pairs of underwear (1 pair for every 2 days, although the style of underwear is up to each astronaut!)

- ☑ 90 pairs of socks (1 pair for every 2 days)

DRESSING IN SPACE

You might be wondering, why does each bit of clothing need to last for so long? Well, clothing isn't washed and reused in space because it would be too difficult to carry enough water to wash clothes. So once their clothing is really dirty, astronauts store it in the cargo vessel, and eventually it is burned up in the Earth's atmosphere, along with any other rubbish. Clothes are worn for longer than they might be on Earth because less energy is used in microgravity, so astronauts typically sweat less. But they might still be smelly! NASA would like a better solution to dirty clothes than burning them up – can you think of some other way of dealing with them?

IS THERE ANYTHING SPECIAL ABOUT ASTRONAUT CLOTHING?

Actually, space clothing is often similar to the clothes you might wear, but with a few extra bits added. Astronauts' work trousers are usually cargo pants with Velcro added, which can be used to stick items to them. Cotton generally isn't used, as it can cause bobbles of lint to fly around the space station, which could get caught in equipment. Shoes aren't really necessary in microgravity, apart from during exercise, so astronauts wear socks most of the time.

* This list is based on a packing list from NASA instructor and engineer Robert Frost. The quantities are worked out based on roughly how many of each item you would need for six months – all numbers are estimates.

WHEN YOU GOTTA GO . . .

When they are in their flight suits, for a spacewalk or take-off and landing, astronauts often wear MAGs (maximum absorbency garments) – in other words, adult-sized nappies! They could be in their suits for hours at a time and might need a wee . . .

On Earth, the way humans use a toilet may vary from country to country, but the result is the same – gravity pulls the waste away from the body, and then it might be flushed away or dirt might be scattered over it. In a microgravity environment in space, humans have to invent different ways to 'flush'.

The latest space loo, updated in 2018, is a vacuum toilet. It has two parts – a hose and funnel, and a seat. You can sit on it or stand over it and place the funnel tightly against you to stop liquids escaping while you wee. To poo, you can sit, using footholds and grabbing hold of handles so you don't float away!

The toilet's suction also stops solid and liquid waste – and smells – from escaping into the space station. Liquid waste (wee) is recycled back into clean drinking water. Solid waste (poo) is put into containers (along with any toilet paper or wipes) and stored in the cargo vessel with the dirty laundry. This load is eventually incinerated in the Earth's atmosphere too. So, sometimes, that 'shooting star' you just glimpsed might actually be frozen astronaut poo burning up in our atmosphere! Would you still make a wish on it?

STRANGER THINGS

As we've just discovered, life for astronauts in space can be pretty strange. Perhaps even stranger is the list of weird and wonderful objects that have gone with them:

- In 1971, Alan Shepard smuggled a ball and golf club inside his spacesuit and on to Apollo 14, so that he could hit a golf ball on the Moon.

- Astronauts have eaten pizzas delivered to the ISS by Pizza Hut aboard a Russian rocket.

- Gorilla suits were also sent to the ISS – astronauts used them to play tricks on each other!

- The Lego company sent three figures to Jupiter on board the Juno spacecraft.

- In 2008, a Buzz Lightyear figure was sent into space, where it spent fifteen months.

- In 2009, the pilot Amelia Earhart's watch was flown to the ISS.

The list of objects to get their astronaut wings also includes: pies and chips, dirt from stadiums, lamb chops, lightsabers, an armchair, slime and even a car!

In 1965, astronaut Walter Schirra Jr used some bells and a harmonica to play a festive trick on mission control. He told them he'd spotted a 'satellite' with a pilot wearing a 'red suit' – before playing 'Jingle Bells' on his harmonica, with his crewmate Thomas Stafford ringing the bells!

THE MANY FACES OF ORION

Orion the Hunter is one of the most well-known 'human' constellations, and has different names and meanings around the world. In Arabic cultures, the stars around the Orion constellation make up a giant, while the Tupi people of Brazil see an old man. Hindus see Orion as a depiction of the god Vishnu. In Australia, an Aboriginal people known as the Wiradjuri see Orion as their creator, Baiame, wielding a shield and a boomerang.

THE
MICROSCOPIC
ASTRONAUTS
INSIDE US

Did you know that the biggest animal and the smallest animal to make it into space so far have travelled there together?

The largest animals to have gone into space to date are humans. And funnily enough, humans grow even bigger when they are in a microgravity environment. Because there is less gravity pulling down on your spine, the bones and cartilage are able to stretch, giving you a few extra centimetres of height! You wouldn't walk tall for long, though – as soon as you were back on Earth, where gravity would exert its usual pull again, you'd shrink back to your original height.

The smallest creatures to have been taken up to space are microbes and bugs. They came along for the ride to show scientists how the microbes inside the human body might fare in a zero-gravity environment. Micro-organisms could prove vital in making sure astronauts are protected from infections in space. And – who knows? – they might even be able to show us where aliens are hiding in our universe – because, believe it or not, while some microbes and bugs have been taken by humans into space, others have actually been found there!

IN SPACE, NO ONE HEARS YOU WHEN YOU THROW UP

It is really important that the astronauts on board the ISS stay healthy. That's why there are lots of rules and regulations around contamination (micro-organisms spreading through touch, for example), as well as close monitoring of the bugs that are either found in space or taken there. Samples of the bugs are taken regularly, and all equipment is cleaned and assembled in sterile rooms before launch. As well as helping to prevent any of the astronauts getting ill, this is also to avoid accidentally taking Earth-based bugs into space and then mistakenly thinking that we've found life there!

There have been some interesting experiments using bugs in space. One showed that the micro-organism that causes food poisoning thrives in space and is three times more likely to cause illness up there. Another bug, *E. coli*, can grow in higher concentrations in space, which is surprising because it was thought that astronauts on the ISS were more resilient to getting ill. A NASA team have found different strains of bacteria on the ISS, including some in the space toilet! Some of these had never been found on Earth – but thankfully none of the unusual types are harmful to the astronauts.

BUGS IN SPACE!

A tough bacterium called *Deinococcus radiodurans* was sent to space, where it thrived for three years on the outside of the ISS! This mighty microbe seemed to be able to withstand microgravity, radiation, the vacuum of space, very high and very low temperatures, freezing and desiccation – when all of its moisture was removed.

IS IT A BUG? IS IT A BEAR? . . .

Tiny bugs called tardigrades, also known as water bears, show amazing qualities in space too. These creatures are about 0.5 mm long and look like a mix between a Shar Pei dog and a piglet, but with eight legs! They are known for being able to survive extreme environments – on Earth, they are found deep in the ocean, in volcanoes, in freezing ice and in the desert.

Tardigrades were first taken into space in 2007 for a ten-day mission. They were dehydrated, then exposed to outer space and solar radiation. When they got back to Earth, they were rehydrated and most of them came back to life, and even reproduced successfully. In fact, tardigrades are so tough that they can live in their dehydrated 'tun' state for several years before being rehydrated, without any damage to their bodies.

In 2019, an Israeli spacecraft, *Beresheet*, crashed into the Moon. The lunar lander contained, among other things, thousands of tardigrades in their tun state. As a result of the accident, thousands of dehydrated water bears might be scattered on the Moon to this day!

We don't know whether the tardigrades could have survived the crash, but if they did, then it's possible they could survive there in their tun state. Maybe when humans next return to the Moon, they'll find lunar tardigrades waiting to be brought back to life!

On Earth, microbes break down organic matter – like rotting leaves – and can be used to make medicines and food, such as bread and yoghurt. Experiments are being carried out on the ISS to find out if microbes could do similar jobs in space. If they are successful, these tiny astronauts could prove very useful on long space missions in the future.

IS THERE LIFE OUT THERE?

Bacteria that can withstand extreme environments on Earth – also known as extremophiles – could be the key to finding life elsewhere in our universe. Deep in our oceans are hydrothermal (hot water) vents, which spurt out water rich in chemicals and minerals that feed the tough bacteria that live there. We already know of under-the-surface ocean habitats on Enceladus (a moon of Saturn) and Europa (a moon of Jupiter). If we could build a spacecraft that could travel to those places, drill through the icy surface and sample the water for bacteria, we might discover that we are not alone in space . . .

ARE THERE ALIENS BEYOND OUR OWN SOLAR SYSTEM?

We have been searching for exoplanets – planets outside our own solar system – since the 1990s, and so far over 5,000 have been found. Some are as big as Jupiter, but much closer to their own star, and therefore much hotter than Jupiter. Others appear to be more like mini-Neptunes, and some are tantalizingly Earth-like. There are other solar systems in the Milky Way galaxy that have up to five planets, but whether these planets could have life on them depends on the distance they are from their star. If the planet is too close to its star, it would be too hot to sustain life. If it is too far away, everything would be frozen. Luckily for us, the Earth's distance from the Sun is just right.

THE GOLDILOCKS ZONE

This area where conditions would be 'just right' for life to exist is called the Goldilocks Zone, taking its name from Goldilocks' fairy-tale quest for the perfect bowl of porridge. In this zone, there is the potential for liquid water to exist on a planet's surface. Because we know the existence of water is essential for life on Earth, if we are searching for life elsewhere in space, locating a water source is a good place to start.

OVER AND OUT

In this book, we've met the tiny but amazing tardigrades that can withstand the harsh environment of space without so much as a spacesuit.

We've learned about the fruit flies that paved the way for bigger creatures to make their way to space, and the gravity-defying spiders that spin their webs up there. We've found out how mighty mice might help us stay healthy in space, and we've been wowed by the not-so-slow-and-steady tortoises who beat humans to the Moon.

We've wondered at real-life space jellyfish – and some galactic ones. Then there were the stray dogs who captured our hearts, not to mention the lone cat who flew too. We've met the monkeys and apes who will go down in history for showing us what we humans might be capable of out there.

And let's not forget the humans who've already been to space, including those who, along with some of the animals, tragically lost their lives during space missions, and those who continue to amaze us with their extraterrestrial adventures. Last but not least, we should mention the microscopic astronauts – the microbes that live inside us and that might even one day be found to exist on other planets as well.

We've seen how all kinds of earthlings, no matter how big or small, can make a huge impact in the world of space discovery. What do you think the next generation of space explorers will go on to discover? Could you be one of them?

Happy
World Book Day!

When you've read this book, you can keep the fun going by swapping it, talking about it with a friend, or reading it again!

What do you want to read next? Whether it's **comics**, **audiobooks**, **recipe books** or **non-fiction** you can visit your school, local library or nearest bookshop for your next read – someone will always be happy to help.

World Book Day is about changing lives through reading

When you **choose to read** in your spare time it makes you

| Feel happier | Better at reading | More successful |

Find your **reading superpower** by

1. Listening to books being read aloud (or listening to audiobooks)
2. Having books at home
3. Choosing the books YOU want to read
4. Asking for ideas on what to read next
5. Making time to read
6. Finding ways to make reading FUN!

SPONSORED BY

NATIONAL BOOK tokens

Changing lives through a love of books and reading.

World Book Day® is a charity sponsored by National Book Tokens

ILLUSTRATED BY VIVIAN TRUONG